# Good Manners

## LUCIA RAATMA

**Children's Press®**
An Imprint of Scholastic Inc.
New York   Toronto   London   Auckland   Sydney
Mexico City   New Delhi   Hong Kong
Danbury, Connecticut

**Content Consultants**

Dave Riley, PhD, is a professor in the Human Development & Family Studies Department at the University of Wisconsin–Madison. Colette Sisco is a faculty member in the psychology department at Madison College, Madison, Wisconsin.

Library of Congress Cataloging-in-Publication Data

Raatma, Lucia.
 Good manners/by Lucia Raatma.
    pages cm—(A true book)
 Includes bibliographical references and index.
 ISBN 978-0-531-25523-0 (lib. bdg.) — ISBN 978-0-531-23923-0 (pbk.)
 1. Etiquette for children and teenagers. I. Title.
 BJ1857.C5R33 2013
 395.1'22—dc23                                                    2012036003

All rights reserved. Published in 2013 by Children's Press, an imprint of Scholastic Inc.
Printed in the United States of America 113
SCHOLASTIC, CHILDREN'S PRESS, A TRUE BOOK™, and associated logos are trademarks and/or registered trademarks of Scholastic Inc.
1 2 3 4 5 6 7 8 9 10 R 22 21 20 19 18 17 16 15 14 13

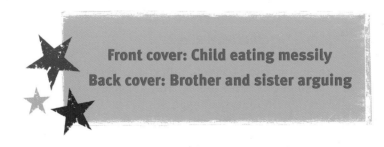

Front cover: Child eating messily
Back cover: Brother and sister arguing

# Find the Truth!

**Everything** you are about to read is true *except* for one of the sentences on this page.

Which one is **TRUE**?

**T or F**  Interrupting other people is okay.

**T or F**  It's important to make eye contact when speaking to other people.

Find the answers in this book.

# Contents

Always say "please" and "thank you" during meals.

# **4** Good Manners on the Playing Field

Shaking hands after a game shows good sportsmanship.

Holding the door open for someone is just one example of good manners.

# CHAPTER 1

# Getting to Know Good Manners

Do you know what having good manners means? In many different ways, it means being **polite** and thoughtful. It means treating other people the way you would like to be treated. It also means thinking before you speak or act. Every day, you can choose to have good manners.

 Try to be polite to everyone you meet each day.

# Bad Manners

Have you ever been treated with bad manners? Think about a time when someone was not polite to you. Perhaps a friend told you to "shut up." Or maybe your big sister used your favorite markers without asking. You probably felt angry—and maybe sad, too. When a person has good manners, he or she considers how other people feel.

It is always polite to ask before taking something that belongs to someone else.

Etiquette is a word that describes proper social behavior.

Can you think of times when you have shown bad manners? Maybe you laughed at a classmate's new haircut. Perhaps you weren't friendly when your cousin came to visit. Or maybe you turned down a dessert by saying to your mom, "No, that looks terrible." How do you think you made those people feel?

A handwritten thank-you note shows you appreciate a person's thoughtfulness.

## Please and Thank You

"Please" and "thank you" are two of the most important phrases in the English language. Do you remember to use them? When you ask for something, say "please." Say "thank you" when you receive something. These simple words let other people know you appreciate what they are doing for you. Then they will be more willing to help you again in the future.

# Other Important Words

If you need to get through a crowd, you can say "excuse me." This is a polite way to let people know you need to get by. This phrase works when you burp or sneeze, too! When someone thanks you for doing something nice, be sure to say "you're welcome." If you need to ask permission, begin with "may I?" And if you really don't want something that is being offered, just say "no, thank you."

Say "excuse me," after you sneeze. If someone else sneezes, you might say "bless you."

# Looking People in the Eye

Make sure that when you speak to others, you look them in the eye. Have you ever said "hello" to someone who didn't say "hello" back? Or did that person mumble "hi" but look at the ground? It probably feels awkward. When you are first introduced to someone, stand up and smile. Say, "Hello. So nice to meet you." A friendly greeting is the best way to start any new friendship.

**Making eye contact shows a person that you're listening and interested in what that person has to say.**

12

# Treating Others Right

Have you ever heard of the Golden Rule? It says that you should treat others the way you'd like them to treat you. Sounds simple enough, right? Every day, no matter what you are doing, consider how your actions affect other people. Would you want other people to **exclude** you from a kickball game? Would you want someone to cut in line in front of you?
Think about it.

Whether your family is big or small, remember to treat every member with respect.

# CHAPTER 2

# Good Manners at Home

When you're at home, you're likely spending time with the people who mean the most to you. Your family may be parents and siblings, as well as stepparents, stepbrothers, and stepsisters. You may live with grandparents, aunts, uncles, and cousins. No matter whom you share a home with, it's important to treat them with kindness and **respect**.

*Respect* comes from the Latin word *respectus,* meaning "to look back at."

# Asking for Permission

Before you borrow your sister's sweater, be sure to ask permission. Would you want her to explore your closet without asking first? That would probably feel like she is invading your **privacy**. The same is true for using your dad's camera or your mom's tennis racket. You may be able to guess that they won't mind, but asking permission first lets them know you'll be using their things.

**Ask permission before borrowing clothes or other items from someone.**

When making plans with a friend, you might have to tell him you'll call him back after you've spoken with your parents.

Always ask permission if you want to have a friend over. Ask permission about going to a party or other event, too. Remember that your parents have your safety in mind. You need to check with them before making any plans. Also, be sure to ask when your friends aren't listening. Your parents will be put in a tough spot if you ask, "Can Tommy stay for dinner?" when Tommy is standing right there.

Respect other people's closed doors. If you need privacy, you can close your door, too.

Be sure to knock softly. Don't bang or shout.

## Closed Doors

Everyone deserves a certain amount of privacy. Never burst into rooms without knocking. A closed door can mean a lot of things. Maybe your brother is taking a shower. Maybe your sister is getting dressed. Or maybe your parents are having a private conversation. Always knock and wait for permission before entering a room.

# Household Chores

There are lots of chores that keep a home running smoothly. Someone must do the laundry, feed the cat, wash the dishes, and take out the garbage. Adults don't always have time to do all those tasks. So remember to do the chores assigned to you. When you have a chance, offer to help out with other things, too. Pitch in with yard work, and help bring in the groceries. Efforts like these show you care.

**Chores can be finished faster if you lend a helping hand.**

# Tone of Voice

Sometimes it isn't what you say, but how you say it. If your mom asks you a question, answer in a polite tone. A grumbled answer or **sarcastic** remark is rude. Remember to speak to others the way you like to be spoken to. Even if you are angry or upset, be careful about how your words sound. If you speak respectfully, other people will be encouraged to speak to you with respect, too.

**Speak calmly and respectfully. Then people will be more willing to listen to what you have to say.**

20

Sometimes you can help a person calm down and feel better just by listening to that person.

# Being a Good Listener

Sometimes it is important to explain a problem or tell your side of a story. But sometimes it is more important to listen. If your parents are upset with you, hear what they have to say. Try not to talk back disrespectfully. When you listen politely and speak calmly, your parents will be more willing to hear your response. If your brother has had a bad day, listen to his complaints. Do not interrupt when others are talking.

You may not see the person you're talking to on the phone or Internet, but the things you say still matter.

# Good Manners on the Internet

These days, many of your conversations may not happen in person. Instead, they may take place through e-mail or text messaging. When you send an e-mail or text, be careful about what you say. Are you teasing someone? Are you replying in anger? Take a minute to review your words before you hit the Send button.

When you e-mail or use **social media** sites, remember that you are talking with real people. Never say something on the Internet that you wouldn't say in person, face-to-face. Have fun, but be kind and thoughtful. Remember that once you have sent a message, you cannot get it back. Do not send something that you will regret later.

Try not to use ALL CAPS when you type messages. Others may think you are SHOUTING!

# Being a Good Neighbor

Whether you live in a house or an apartment, you probably have neighbors. These are people who live around you. Some you might see once a week. Others you might see every day. Good neighbors are people you can count on. They may help you in an emergency. Or they might invite you to a party they are hosting.

**You probably see your neighbors on a pretty regular basis.**

**If a neighbor looks like he needs a hand with something like groceries, you can offer to help out.**

One way to be a good neighbor is to respect other people's property. Don't cut through their yard or leave your toys in their grass. Never steal anything that belongs to them. Be careful of their plants and flowers. You can also show **courtesy** by helping them out when you can. Offer to rake their leaves. Hold the door open when they are carrying packages. They will appreciate your help.

# Good Manners Matter Every Day

When you go out for lunch with family or friends, how do you act? Remember to treat everyone around you with respect. That includes your friends and family, the other people eating there, and the people working at the restaurant. Keep these tips in mind:

When talking to restaurant servers, be polite. Speak clearly, and use the words *please* and *thank you*.

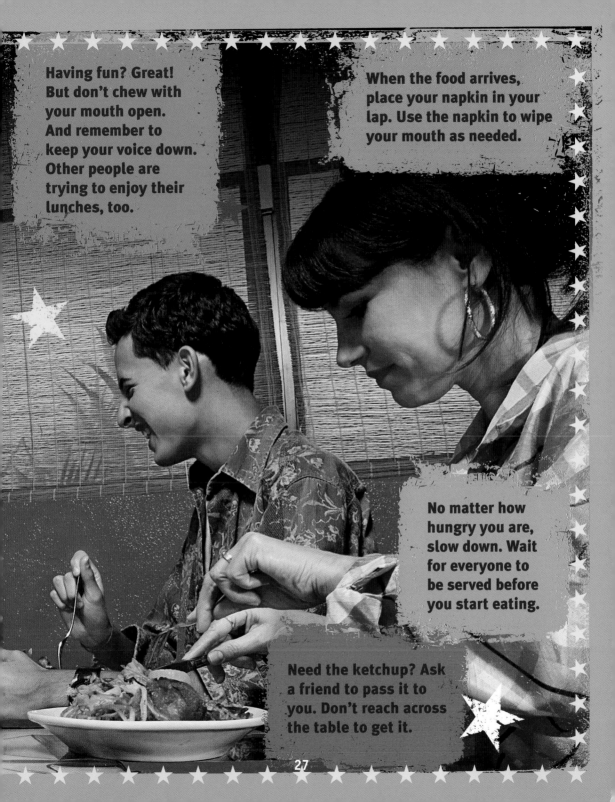

Having fun? Great! But don't chew with your mouth open. And remember to keep your voice down. Other people are trying to enjoy their lunches, too.

When the food arrives, place your napkin in your lap. Use the napkin to wipe your mouth as needed.

No matter how hungry you are, slow down. Wait for everyone to be served before you start eating.

Need the ketchup? Ask a friend to pass it to you. Don't reach across the table to get it.

27

When your teacher or another student is speaking, be sure to stay quiet and listen.

# CHAPTER 3

# Good Manners at School

How much time do you spend in school? If you're like most kids, it's almost half a day. You probably have some good friends there. You might also have a favorite teacher or two. It's important to use good manners with the people you see at school every day. This is true whether those people are your best friends or other students you don't know very well.

 Smile at your classmates to encourage them when they are presenting to the class.

# Showing Respect

Your teachers work hard to help you learn. They help you prepare for projects, tests, and future classes. Make sure you treat them well. Use those magic words *please* and *thank you* when asking for things. Listen during class. Raise your hand before speaking. And always ask permission before leaving your classroom for any reason. Helping to create a polite, respectful classroom makes it easier for everyone to concentrate and learn.

**Raise your hand before asking a question or giving an answer in class.**

**Cafeteria workers keep lunchtime running smoothly.**

Teachers are not the only adults at school. You probably also see adults in the cafeteria and the main office. Be polite to these people, too. They work hard to make sure you have everything you need. They serve lunch, clean up classrooms, and help keep you safe. Never talk disrespectfully to them or **taunt** them. Instead, take time to say "hello" and thank them every once in a while!

Getting teased or bullied is hurtful and can make school a scary place to be.

## How You Treat Other Kids

Are there any bullies at your school? These kids tease other kids. They can make school days hard for everyone. Make sure you aren't a bully. Don't joke about what another student looks like. Never exclude other kids on the playground. Instead, smile at your classmates. Offer help when they need it. If you treat other kids with respect and kindness, they'll likely treat you the same way.

Bullies sometimes make fun of people using social media. They might post videos about other kids. They may also spread **gossip** on Facebook and other sites. These actions can hurt people's feelings. They might even keep kids from coming to school or having friends. If you know this is happening, talk to an adult about it.

Talk to someone if you or a friend is being bullied. Friends, parents, teachers, and other trusted people can help you figure out what to do.

# Good Manners on the Playground

During recess or your lunch break, you probably love being on the playground. You get to play with your friends and have fun. But remember that good manners matter there, too. Don't cut in line if others are waiting for the swings or the slide. Invite other kids to join your game of kickball or tag. And be sure to listen to the adults who are watching you.

# Good Manners Timeline

### 1922

**Emily Post, famous for writing about manners, publishes the best seller _Etiquette in Society, in Business, in Politics, and at Home._**

### 1991

**The Institute for International Sport creates National Sportsmanship Day.**

# Working Hard

Because you are young, you may not think you have a real job. But you do. Your job is to go to school and learn as much as you can. This means being responsible, listening in class, and studying. It means doing your homework. It also means that you never cheat. Cheating on homework or on tests is a version of stealing. And it is never nice or proper to steal from other people.

**2004**
**Facebook is launched as a social media site. In 2012, it had more than 900 million users.**

**2011**
**On March 10, the White House holds its first Conference on Bullying Prevention.**

Win or lose, you should always try to be a good sport.

# CHAPTER 4

# Good Manners on the Playing Field

Do you play team sports? Maybe you compete in dancing, karate, or other activities. These are great ways to stay active and fit. To be successful, you have to practice and play hard. Some days, you will win. Other days, you won't. Either way, these activities can still be fun. To make it fun for everyone, be sure to practice good manners.

 A good sport can handle both winning and losing.

# Being a Good Sport

You are a good sport when you approach every competition in a positive way. You try your best. You encourage your teammates to do their best, too. A good sport does not hog the ball or need to be the center of every play. Instead, a good sport works with his or her teammates to make each game fun.

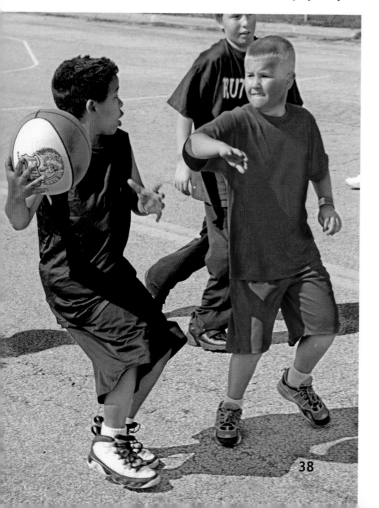

**Basketball and other sports are more fun when teammates work together.**

It is important to learn from mistakes.

**Everyone makes mistakes sometimes.**

What if you make a mistake? Do you throw the ball down and walk away? Do you kick your water bottle? Do you cry and pout? No, of course not. You should take responsibility for making a mistake. Think about what you did wrong and how to do better. Then realize it's time to try harder.

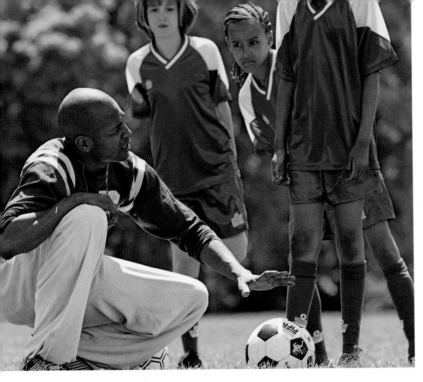

You can learn a lot from your coach.

# Showing Respect

When you play a sport, you rely on your coaches to help you become better. These adults work to teach you and help you improve. You show good manners when you listen to your coaches and follow their directions. You also show good manners when you come to practices and games on time. Showing up late could mean you miss the chance to play.

During a competition, there are other adults you should listen to as well. These can be referees, umpires, and other officials. They are there to keep the competition fair and running smoothly. You may not like every call they make. But a good sport accepts the call. It never helps to yell at a referee or umpire. Show good manners by treating your teammates, coaches, and referees with respect.

**It might be tough to accept a referee's call.**

# A Good Winner and a Good Loser

When you lose a game or competition, you might take it hard. But part of being a good sport is being a good loser. Accept that you didn't win this time. Congratulate the other team on a good game.

What if you win? Enjoy the moment! But don't ever brag. Remember that other people lost. You don't want to hurt their feelings. Instead, tell them they did a good job and encourage them for next time.

Even when you are frustrated, try to treat people with respect. Then they will be more likely to help you solve whatever issue is ruining your day.

## Manners Always Matter

It can sometimes be difficult to practice good manners. You might become frustrated with yourself, other kids, or the adults around you. When you play in a game or competition, some people may be negative. But even when you are upset, it is important to be polite and respectful. When you act maturely and responsibly, kids will enjoy your company. Adults will treat you with respect. It is always worth it to show good manners! ★

**Number of Americans who think lack of respect and courtesy is a national problem:** 8 out of 10

**Percentage of students who see bullying as an ongoing problem:** More than 70

**Number of middle schoolers who have had their feelings hurt online:** 9 out of 10

**Number of Americans (of any age) who report getting rude or nasty e-mails:** 4 out of 10

**Percentage of people who believe the world would be a better place if everyone said "please" and "thank you" more often:** 85

**Percentage of Americans who admit to acting rude or disrespectful:** More than 40

**Percentage of people who believe that sportsmanship is the most important part of the youth sports experience:** 84

**Percentage of people who believe that coaches should encourage good sportsmanship over winning:** 97

## Did you find the truth?

**F** Interrupting other people is okay.

**T** It's important to make eye contact when speaking to other people.

# Resources

## Books

Espeland, Pamela, and Elizabeth Verdick. *Dude, That's Rude!* Minneapolis: Free Spirit Publishing, 2007.

Post, Peggy, and Cindy Post Senning. *Emily Post's Table Manners for Kids*. New York: Collins, 2009.

Post, Peggy, and Cindy Post Senning. *Emily Post's The Guide to Good Manners for Kids*. New York: HarperCollins Publishers, 2004.

**Visit this Scholastic Web site for more information on good manners:**
www.factsfornow.scholastic.com
Enter the keywords **Good Manners**

# Important Words

**courtesy** (KUR-ti-see) — well-mannered behavior

**exclude** (ik-SKLOOD) — to keep someone from joining a group or taking part in something

**gossip** (GOSS-ip) — idle talk about other people's personal business

**polite** (puh-LITE) — having good manners; being well behaved and courteous

**privacy** (PRYE-vuh-see) — the state of belonging to or concerning one person or group and no one else

**respect** (ri-SPEKT) — a feeling of admiration or high regard for someone or something

**sarcastic** (sahr-KAS-tik) — bitter or mocking, intending to hurt or make fun of someone or something

**social media** (SOH-shuhl MEE-dee-uh) — Web sites that help people connect with each other

**taunt** (TAWNT) — to try to make someone angry or upset by saying unkind things about him or her

# Index

Page numbers in **bold** indicate illustrations.

# About the Author

Lucia Raatma is a writer and editor who enjoys working on books for young readers. She earned a bachelor's degree in English from the University of South Carolina and a master's degree in cinema studies from New York University. She likes writing about all sorts of subjects including history, conservation, wildlife, character education, and social media. She lives with her husband and their two children in the Tampa Bay area of Florida.